House of Burnt Offerings

House of Burnt Offerings

Judith Skillman

Cover art by Mira Lehr, *Angel Hair*, 18"x23"
Woodblock, hand drawing, ink, collage and burnt paper,
2010

Author photo by Thea Billings

Layout and design by Chris Yeseta

ISBN 978-0-912887-32-6
Library of Congress Control Number: 2015933394

This is a collection of poems, works of the imagination,
not documents of actual fact or historical or biographical
accuracy, so any resemblance to actual persons living or dead
is but coincidence.

First U.S. Printing

PLEASURE BOAT STUDIO: A LITERARY PRESS
www.pleasureboatstudio.com
201 West 89th Street
New York, NY 10024
Website: *www.pleasureboatstudio.com*
e-mail: *pleasboat@nyc.rr.com*

Pleasure Boat Studio books are available through your
favorite bookstore and through **SPD** (Small Press Distribution),
Partners/West, Baker & Taylor, Ingram, Brodart, Amazon.com,
and **bn.com** and also through our website via credit card.

for my daughters,
Alissa Regen Tuininga
&
Jocelyn Ann Skillman

Acknowledgements

Thanks to these journals, where the following poems first appeared, some in different versions:

"The Turnip," *A Minor Magazine*

"The Child's Pose," "In Squalor," "Burnt Offering," *Hubbub*

"Wand," *Narrative Northeast*

"Vases of Peonies," "The Rustling," *Tampa Review Online (TRON)*

"Swaybacked," "House of Burnt Cherry," *The Pedestal Magazine*

"This Sadness is No One's," *The Kentucky Review*

"Cicada," *Cirque*

"Kafka's Wound," *The Portland Review*

"Jobless," *Floating Bridge Press Review*

"Die Kinder," *Barnwood*

"Ah Vallejo," *Kentucky Review*

"Skunked," "The Young Widow," *Strong Verse*

"Mis en Abyme" *The Chiron Review*

"Winter Burlesque," *Message in a Bottle*

"The Green Hour," *Lantern Journal*

"Lethe as Mass," *Deep Water Literary Journal*

"Israel," "Semitic," *The Raven Chronicles*

"Lisa's Dress," *Colorado-North Review*

"Hashimoto's Disease," "Placebo," *Journal of the American Medical Association (JAMA)*

"The Succulents," *St. Katherine's Review*

"Atonement," *Poetica Magazine*

"Moods and Qualities," *J Journal,* John Jay School of
    Criminal Justice

"Windfall," *Willows Wept Review*

"Crabapples," *Poetry Northwest*

"In the Dog House," *Iconoclast*

"Restraint," *Compass Rose*

"The Train" appeared in the anthology *Fault Lines.*

"Goaded" appeared in the 2015 *Poet's Market*

Cover artist Mira Lehr is a multimedia artist whose work
spans four decades. She is best known for her nature-based
imagery. She is represented by The Flomenhaft Gallery in
New York and The Kelley Roy Gallery in Miami.

Thanks to colleagues Gayle Kaune and Tina Kelley for their
assistance with the manuscript.

All gratitude to fellow poets Christianne Balk, Irene Bloom,
Pat Hurshell, Susan Sigrun Lane, Carol Ruth Kelly, Anne
Pitkin, Diane Ray, Joannie Stangeland, Mary Ellen Talley,
and Lillo Way.

Contents

3.

—1—

We struggle to thread ourselves through the eye of a needle,
Face to face with the desires.

César Vallejo, *Trilce XXXVI*

The Turnip

Once more you force
its fisted mass. Blanched white
with a feather of pink—
the bloodless promise?
Has the chemistry of want
exploded the dreamy cluck
of that heart in your chest?
Under the sky, the grave
of dawn's planted again—
its beginning wed
to the same milky stone.

The Child's Pose

Never the children we wanted to be,
we ran away, sat on porches, hobos
holding sticks with makeshift bags.

Unable to stop the arguments, we left,
returning only when hunger crept too close.
Huddled alone, salt in our throats—

that telltale taste infected our thin clothing.
Scared to return a boxed ear, a hard pinch,
or the tickling torture of relatives, we began

to learn, like peasants, all over again,
how to finger an amulet of red beads.
Evil, when kept at bay, seemed almost good.

Then rain whet our appetites for heartsickness
and we grew up. A big wind came, trees blew
unfettered, their branches lifting as if

to reveal, beneath green skirts, what it was
had to be hidden from all the eye-lamps
that lit up our bright brothels

of emotion. Were we objects attached like chairs
to table? Had we fallen asleep after eating
the best dreams in the house?

Wand

If there's a synonym for magic
        it lies not in the wand
but at the bud-bent end.

The body's a spring,
        the mind a whore.
Easter dawn, and loss.

Better to have been born poor
        than come to this late poverty
where milk carries its aftertaste

and what's been bought and sold—
        orchid from the realtor—
decorates a scarred teak table.

Better to have been made
        to make do all along:
then she unwrapped a stick of butter,

saved the wrapper to smear a pan
        for the next flat cake
taken from the cavern of her oven.

Old moon-faced clock
        just beginning to light
the humble kitchen

where each day began
        at the same stained bowl:
then she wore her torn robe

over white bra and underwear,
        a dateless slip,
four dresses that carried through

every season. Lavender in a vase
        on the Formica table,
its smart yellow chairs.

Vases of Peonies

We bring them in heavy
from the garden, we carry their weight
in our arms as if their pinks
were flesh. An atmosphere is created
inside the house exclusively of scent—
bridal, nuptial, called to order.

Their ruffled crinolines last for a day
and they become tow-headed girls
rallying for a fight, and they become
the spiders in their rose-wings, the ants
walking quickly away from.

We bring and bring them in
as if such a thing as a bouquet
could be painted by the unknown artist
who rents our nonexistent attic.

As if the head, the luxurious arm of green—
outstretched, having slept the sleep
of languor in the yard after bursting
from dark soil—as if even one
of these perfect Persephones
could live among our interruptions
and gallant intrusions, the sharp shears
of our smiling teeth.

Swaybacked

I enter the animal called self.
Its bones no longer quite aligned.

I ride the animal in the direction
of dressage, put on my posture.

I call myself *Madame* when others say *Ma'am*,
their accents of the deep south preserved
like shrunken heads in formaldehyde.

I enter the bird called voice.
Its trill resembles the fishwife
who nags those close to her with curses
      & compulsions.

I enter the weather titled Spring.
Cherry petals accumulate like snow on the patio,
where self & voice design ruffled birds & bloodless queries.

Where does the airplane go close to supper?
How do lilacs send scent into the windows of neighbors?
Shall I procure, from milk, butter, & a bit of flour,
the white sauce my mother taught me how to make
when I came of age?

I enter the light called dusk.
All the symbols of youth swallow, swallowed by Eliot's violets.
Tiresius—even Prufrock, who hardly knew whether to eat
      the bloody peach.

I enter my spine as question mark.

This Sadness is No One's

It belongs to the white chicken,
and the child-woman
whose mother had fetal alcohol syndrome,
to the gray hulk of sky.

It is neither yours nor mine,
nor the woman who works
in the bakery or the post office
or the jewelry store.

This sadness lingers in a tone
of wood, in trains bulleting
from east to west.
It is vacancy enlarged with winter.

What you hold
isn't warm or alive. It doesn't cluck,
pick grubs from mud,
or strut around the yard

as if to impress.
This is the solitary watch.
Take the gun, the magnet,
the trick of hands without cards.

Cicada

When you were born
the veined wings came.

Such large eyes
you said, and the answer

came—*all the better
to see through darkness.*

Translucent wings beat
back your childhood

as certain dreams grew transparent—
the strong back,

arms ready to carry infant-others.
When the time came

the wretch had red eyes
and leather skin. So much drama

behind the set
of any fairy tale—*Midsummer Night's Dream,*

Our Town. Afterward
husks littered the ground

like empty soda cans.
When you were born

the play contained a lecher,
an ignorant mother,

an absent father.
Such big hands

you said, and the answer
came—*all the better*

to break a girl.
A hail of shells fell

for the thread that ties
one generation to the next:

a knot that can't be undone.
Embroidered blackness

and the pimp in the tree,
his white, drumlike plates

singing, the thrum
of abdomens filling

the sky with mating
calls. Then to lie

drunk on death
and other shrouded visions.

Kafka's Wound

Toward sunset it bleeds orange, plums,
and wine. His father always at table
with mug in hand. How long
must a son allow the city to unwind
its long avenues, branching rivers

full of walkers insular with autumn.
It's true the blade took garlic cloves
from their little white coats,
so pliant, the stems beneath that fat knife
wolfing into the core of the matter.

It's true there must be a mother
in the story—her stringy hair, her roast
burning in the oven. He sees the clock tower
in the square, glances up to find a rim of moon.
At least, for now, the hole's been bled

of what it holds. As far as a man can walk
the shops stretch, their signs reversed.
Closed for another, longer night.
Withholding exactly that porcelain—
that *Jan Becher Karlovy* liqueur cup

one needs to clamp between finger
and thumb. He's learned one lesson.
This wound must be purged each day.
Else the stench of what it carries
emanates from his mouth, and others turn away.

Skunked

When the window's open,
fan sucking air from a swath
of wetland. Before the ink
has dried on the contract for a house
you decide to buy.

The upstairs floor creaks.
There's always a man
upstairs, something to do
with numbers and spectra.
From the argument of scents

a yellow cloud wafts.
The wasp hotel full now,
and each type of meat
attracting more tuxedos.
A bit of cheese dropped from a sandwich,

a star falling to earth, burning up
in its own white streak.
The space station on time,
magnitude far brighter
than Venus. It has to happen

several times in one lifetime—
the embarrassment of public
speaking, preceded or followed
by insomnia. What else has been waiting
at the peripheries of the season:

accident, mislaid glasses, girl who sat on a bee
while recovering from rheumatic fever?
It will happen that someone
who loved you becomes
a millionaire, and you—

the friend of his ex-wife—
must spend time listening
to trains, hearing that plaintive wail
of those who once traveled from east to west.
You must sit alone

in the stink and blush
of remembrance,
in the stammer of household names,
loading separate compartments
for spoon, fork, and knife.

Comes the Solstice

Yet somehow the moon
remains only a mirror.
Meant to reflect, as we
do at the worst
times of our lives,
something larger,
more angry than we are.
The sun—no more terrestrial
than tape grass. A star
holding four rocky globes
in orbit, a furnace whose desserts
glint from water, windows,
and the brown eyes
of my father, who studied
its flares and prominences
even as he raged against
the casserole dishes
placed before him
when the cancer grew
larger than his own
esophagus—the formal
source of all his pleasure.

Die Kinder

Coming from right and left
tent-skirted all night dreaming of

how many like hyenas braying
scuffing dirt
magic-eyed to the *no*
sidewise to the *no*
> the juvenile smile of a pumpkin

> the orange fear
until I am on a par with
of an age the same as jealousy
buying everything with nothing

not pretending in my clothes
my double chins
how childish the dotage
the hose pulled up

> belly fat with failing
muscle tone as auntie's wheeled
into the garden
given another can of *Ensure*

come closer to dreams
where tall flights of stairs
make labyrinths and tunnels

Lethe-winged
meeting dogs
        shaking hands with
the other in green envy
deep killing where the coming rough on
        hoards of sunny dollars

singing through tree leaves
about to brown over
        as with infections
of the inner ear

Displacement

Rain soaks the fields.
Close in,
mustard-colored wall.
In the distance,
the gabled Victorian
mansion—a hive
for old residents
who have given up
on their yards.

Between courtyard
and parklands
a volleyball net,
with white
gauze selvage.
A girl will bruise
her arm to serve.

Behind each separate
scene, tears
accumulate, ready
to answer this rain,
this vague day
full of myriad
grays, tasks, and moods.

The Rooster

Those who romanticize morning
hear it only at dawn.

The ones who suspect foods of poison
listen for it after the hour of noon.

And some betray their lovers
just to revel in its old song

sung on commission in the territories
of spring, oh yes, after sunset.

Ariel Commands

If you think I freed you from the tree
only to have you master my minutes
with rare speeches and harsh orders—
if you dare try that alchemy
without first consulting the oracle
who lives apart from your image
of yourself as little god and hero
come to implement strategies, to write up
here what couldn't be done on land—
well, I am under your aegis despite
my lack of form. Go on then, try to harness
an elemental. Stare me down.
Wrestle me with your ugly, veined hand
and I will fight towards the shore,
for I alone can swim the distance
from this compartment bordered on every side
by water, and I would be thought fair
by any brother who came from the woman
who birthed you, who thought of you
as gentle and kind, well brought up
in art as in the science of planets, orbs,
and droplets of mercury, in which—heavier
than you I daily bathe, and learn
by listening to those birds bearing
what is left of land—feather, talon, claw.

Day Moon

I have blunt-thumbed it out of the sky.
I've taken it upon myself to test its tired shining.

Not that I could live without my sister winter,
or the iron in my veins.

Nor could I count the days
until the cycle ends again as it has before.

Insensible planetoid governing the tides,
pulling earth into shape, twin-mooned one

running through yards between the dorms
in Westminster, hooting naked.

I have remembered the past, taken it upon myself
to live prior to the future—

that friend I never met, for whom I have no desire,
that ball of crystal in which a face shivers.

The Train

Comes on its tracks of bronze and wood ties
carrying the dead,
carrying the living—
a cargo of trash
instead of diners.

Comes the train on its twin tracks of silver
angled into the distance,
perpendiculars growing dark.

I am on the train
watching two young women
talk, laugh, and flirt.

I crochet my childhood.
It falls like cream into my lap.
I make the same shawl over and over
but it never warms me
or keeps me from harm.

Comes the train to Montreal, to Paris,
out of the chalk cities
headed straight for those lands
ripe for picking,
and into the ghetto
to find a miscellany of Jews and Gypsies.

Whistle trembling,
fraught with meaning.
Comes the train into sickness

to succor the ill who will not get well.
On this train babies claw
at their mother's breasts
and all is barren,
the milk crusted dry
in a century full of dross and wailing.

Jobless

My husband rocked
four years
in his little boat on the land,
lost in the strawberry patch.
His fingers calloused,
hands stained with dirt,
he worked close to earth,
made not a dollar,
befriended no one,
and was no one's friend.
Only the rocks—
glacial till—kept company.
He managed
their smooth sides,
hefted them
into the other half
of the acre. One day
he painted black borders
on window moldings.
Another he filled holes
with dirt the mole
had heaped up
from its tunnels, entrances,
and exits. The strawberries
put out runners. These
pale ribbons

my husband inserted
carefully into dirt,
as if braiding
the mane of a horse,
or testing a patch of ice
to see whether
it would hold his weight.

Ah Vallejo,

After you left Peru forever,
you made of guano *Trilce*,
that stands on the border
of every season.

The brick of time
sits between us.
I hold these pages
with the pure love
of a Hippodamia.

Drunken centaurs
come to abduct me.
They break me in two
in two as if I were
a simple straw.

Here on the island
of October, I mimic you
by copying your sadness.

Vallejo your materials remain
exiled as in a gallery
or a prison, those you
painted with terracotta
in the fine oils
of your Thursday.

—2—

Second degree burn
in desire's every tender excrescence,
spike of vagrant hot chili,
at two in the immoral afternoon....

César Vallejo, *Trilce XXX*

Mis En Abyme

A term originally from French, meaning "placing into infinity."

I came to be here, small and hard.
　　　　Like the core—not of an apple, rather
　　　　　　　　wooden as a Russian politician.

　　　　An onion rested on the counter.
　　　　　　Inside it other onions.

The end tables in that muggy-colored living room
　　　　held other end tables.

But let's go back to my desire that you should read the story
　　　　of my dissolute family.

Yes, you should know
what went on at the edge of ideals
　　　　unraveling even as Mother
　　　　　　pleaded with the machine,
its tension and errata.

Pressing seams open with the beak of the iron,
　　　　she would mutter curses
　　　　　　as steam grew into a cauliflower cloud.

This was her peculiar gift—
     the zigzag stitch.

As in the fractal—take
     the *Koch* snowflake, for instance, one of a gazillion
meted out by the sky.

Or frost crystals on cold glass,
     the Mandelbrot set,
         broccolini.

     *

I came to know the child despite
     her refusal to be anything but ill.
Each birthday another case of strep throat.

You must know the *matryoshka*—that is to say, maternal—instinct.

I had children of my own.
They had children.
Sometimes twins as improbable
     as if we were living in a tank of watery sounds
        with the fish-glint of doppelganger.

The doll in my stomach,
      her Easter-painted apron
            and red red smile.

                  *

Who was Father with his viola,
      his tics and grunts, his bow?
            Swipes of with marcato and staccato
      against the Hawaiian wood of his best viola.

Finally you must understand I began with a half size violin, progressed
      to three-quarters, held the whole
            only after years of study
returned me to the state
      of lunatic beginner.

For in the regime of communism, Perestroika
      is always begun too late
            to undo the rule of neurosis.

Passing on the Right

Blue herons in a crease of green
beside the highway, bald eagle
stationed in nondescript tree.
The farmer's house shredded
      by wind,
his crops blunt, shadow-tinged.

This our car, this our winter tongue.
Where miles change to kilometers
we take our cue
      from speed,
leave the border for other roads
beside which Anna Karenina's house
        sat out
the 20th century with no interruption.

Gauze curtains drawn,
blinds pulled,
      light the affect
of rooms never touched
by moon or sun.

In this, the difficult marriage—
      a peripheral glimpse
serves to show how,
well-ordered, evenly spaced

in rows and columns,
still the farmer's crop lies fallow.

If bulbs lie fisted
          deep beneath
glazed ice, they're certain
to hold entire skins
          swaddled, encrusted,
vein-laced and finely traced
by the kind of dirt no snow
will ever see.

House of Burnt Cherry

after William Logan's "Paris in Winter"

Here the martyr and the porcupine
live together, for here they both belong.
Cross the foyer, see two huddled shapes
planted on the sofa ages ago,
bled of light. Come from the Old World,

the spine hog and the one who suffers
torture. Long after midnight the trough
of desire—dry-needled, rotten—leaves
its bee sting on Saint Sebastian.
Here wallpaper peels back the psalms. Scents

of musk rise from stained upholstery.
A rodent's stiff, coarse hairs line the martyr's
back, interspersed with red markings,
where sharp quills dug in pretty *zzz's*
of memory and sleep. Dreams he never

forgets, incidents inscribed on skin.
Beams laid log-cabin style: an outpost
avoided by mailman and assassin,
milk maid and village idiot.
No wonder they hardly get along—

two hogs snuffling at sills to find a bit
of seed. Two states underscored by need.
Two almost-persons married to pity's
cousin, guilt. Like twins who nestle
in the womb, they take up whatever room

yields. Fetal position, hands covering ears.
Oxygen finds a way to enter.
Wasn't the umbilical a channel,
the stink of wood freshened by a blade,
the moon put out by its own candled-wound.

The New Mother

She stands on her deck smoking, leaning
on those lovely arms. *How is he,* we ask,
passing, nostalgia welling up
for our lost chunky ones. She stands
and smokes, steeped in her hair,

her face, her jeans. *He's good, his Dad
came home late and took him for a walk.*
The secret's out, she can't put it back
but she does. *I'm fine until 5 but after that,
well, it's like always being touched,*

I can't even pee without—
We interrupt, our late middle-aged laughter
gnawing at what's left of September summer.
I remember, I say, I was always ready to—
looking sidewise at a man

I barely remember marrying.
Glancing up at the loveliness of her,
all the elements of her home lit
by the kitchen beyond, its canisters
where mystery blends and foments.

I'm fine until 5, she repeats with a faint smile
like the day moon, and we turn away,
see the father heading downhill, the stroller
and blanketed cargo, its selvages
burning like skin meant to be taken

and taken again. That night
we make love until we fall back
in faded blue sheets
sated with too much—*like a finger always
touching you*, she said, *it's like that.*

Hashimoto's Disease

I dreamt a trunk
came down from the ceiling—
      wrinkled and gray
as an elephant's.

      It entered small,
innocuous, as a plant
pokes a shoot through soil.

Others in the room—
the son, the daughter—
      had returned as young
to the fold.

I was to leave
notes for them
about their breakfast,
yet the son persisted in eating
      bear claws.

The trunk became larger,
      waving itself
like the flag of some symbol
I would have to decipher
when I came
      from the state
of sleep to another long day

waging war
against this new diagnosis.

Again, the intruder—
majestic, horrific
as it overtook
          the dining room—
proclaiming, gesticulating.

Like an organ gone awry.
          As when the body
          attacks itself—
I thought, upon waking.

Father, Figure

He takes small things,
tells secrets. Tells me.

The sun sweats under his gaze.
Its spots emerge to magnetize the earth.

He plants an observatory.
Stars whisper, the moon swells.

He takes note of the smallest numbers.
Writes a sheaf of decimal points.

I am punished for giddiness,
for being a girl instead.

In the garden. In the gazebo.
Beside the antique telescope—

its locks and chains, its clock drive.
He talks with the frog in his throat.

Lightens the load of items I borrow
from stores, my hands close to my purse.

My father leaves discreetly, after midnight.
He leaves abruptly in daylight.

He departs after dinner on a plane
bound for Copenhagen, the nexus of affairs.

Winter Burlesque

The birds, their small bright humors,
bleats, notes, masks
        as they swirl about the house.

A sky ruined by rain.
The whirr of small planes,
pampas grass in straw air:
        all light & airy
as a place that hasn't seen tragedy.

~

Three yellow apples
        hang as in dementia
upon the tree, its last leaves scraped clean
        by four winds.

~

This bird, & this, & this,
thrice happy, their own *Burleske*—
Strauss performed
        in nook & cranny.

The willow emptied of tear-shaped leaves,
the wires hung with pigeoned iridescence.

When to break off?
When spare a bright, high-spirited mood
for one's lover, when all's dressed down—
      lake gray, sky gray,
the mood closed, remote?

I stared down the barrel of a gun, he said.

~

A bulky bird, buff-breasted, fine streaking.
Abrupt, well-spaced notes—
two high, ear-bursting.
      A whistle,
then *choo choo choo*, three in a row,
ended with the song bird's amen: a trill.

~

& the land beneath the land—
a sewer of water
running catacombed
      through Lethe's redundant rivers.

The great hall of winter, its drowned
Ophelia arranged in portraiture.
      Face up.

~

Mossed rooftops,
suburbia besieged,
     as Ben stands
below water in *The Graduate,*
wearing scuba gear.

     Another reaper?
Youth this time.

Take these shells away, he said.

~

Ear the unceasing.
Dirge-drum, thrum of water pooling in eaves,
sifting through gutters, rheumy droplets
     on greened wood.

The Green Hour

One to go and workday's finished,
smudged like droplets against
the window. Who else craves
anise-flavored spirits of Grande wormwood,
sweet fennel, la fée verte?

Van Gogh, Verlaine, Baudelaire, Rimbaud
gathered in cafés to toast
the green fairy, her garters mussed
to better hold Artemis' long-legged
beauty. Poor petite absinthe-nymphet

bird of five o' clock intermission
from office, bank, shop, boulangerie.
Wearing clothes she's stolen
from the milliner. A loiterer who learns
nothing, an eye silted with sun.

When did the rhythm of raindrops
leave the weaver? The sound of songs
keep the young from whimsy?
All pastorals praise Pan, and he gone
with syrinx, goats, sheep—run overland.

By Winter

I mean we were melted,
albeit not so casually
as by a handshake.
Iced boughs cracked.
The continual shushing
of compacted snow,
the kraken walking on the roof,
stumbling in its scales,
the horned crows circling…

It's the ping of icicles
made our marriage
come apart.
However simply it dissolved.
Notes of birds
cordoned in the yard,
and the cribbage board's
long-abandoned ivory pegs
shining like the white eyes
of the kraken
when it fell off the house
at last and we could sleep again.

Semitic

Born so. So to speak.
Taken away from the knowledge
of what that meant. So Bess grew up,
overweight, never knowing how to make babies.

They told me that story over and over.
Never told me how to make babies,
nor how to visit Auschwitz—my mother sat outside
and knitted on her cable sweater.

And Father? He threw off the Hebrew
forced like a fishbone down his throat,
where the gutturals stuck. Went entirely
over to the side of science: atheism.

Kept misogyny as if it were a special present
he'd been afforded by virtue of his own neglected childhood.
These things I was given—how not to finger them?
Even an abacus demands to be counted.

What of the flat beads, ringed like Saturn.
Or the belt we were beaten with for certain sins.
That word sin: I had never heard of it.
Nor other words like Jesus.

It's almost Passover again, after all.
I can give up bread for Lent
and call it matzo—what else is a communion wafer
but a bit of matzo taken between the lips

pressed to the roof of the mouth
where it melts luxuriously as if it were the crumb
a starving Jew in Baden Baden saved
in his striped pajama pocket, for a moment

when the guard looked the other way?

Wifery

As stiffly bound to the other
as our hearth and home,
we find ourselves like Hera
in a den of jealous words
and deeds.

We offer the nag's head
a sunset, a good book,
or a meal of cut glass,
explaining how
water freezes and ice thaws.

We find the days
last longer than the light.
Our chain is like that tool
grinding against metal
across the street,

where a man who lost his wife
begins another project.
We know in our dreams
who it is our partner
wishes to sleep with—

a woman like the weather,
whose hair shakes
out blonde coins,
disturbs the darkness.

Lethe as Mass

We were wild florets,
edging from
the water as ripples
and foam signets.

I was of a mind
to leave this doubt,
to crawl single
into doublet

with my carrot-like spikes,
my skeleton of spurs.
The sun is ray
and disks —

it is one thing
when you're young,
another when
they—your old mothers—

come and beckon.
I saw them
as you did, waving
from the far shore.

Nothing precious
as a golden dog—
no coin, not a sign
of *rimon*.

I'm saying you
go flat as a flounder
in the underground
with the feathered roots

left by that mole
who haunted the body,
its passageways
and labyrinths.

Placebo

I have taken the pill of dreams
under winter's dead-pan sky.

The crow flies as it flies, measuring
the distance between a thought

and a spasm. How will I know
the clinic of deception? Pigeons sit

on wires. When the hawk comes
they rise as one bird, duped, circling—

flocking behavior—before settling
back into the danger zone.

Next come smaller swarms:
chits, hatchlings, wrens, finches,

nuthatch, titmouse, swallow, bunting.
A disease can be pinked, ruffled,

twirled by summer winds.
A harmless pill: *his Aunt Bessie*

had been kept alive on sympathy
and placebos for thirty years…

All diseases finite but in memory,
where, once tripped, anxiety wires

the limbic system for another kind
of pain. Its namesake: *chronic.*

Have I lost the use of any limbs?
Will I remember, after swallowing

another capsule, tonic, oil, herb,
how many birds migrate by instinct—

the Bar-headed Goose plowing furrows
above the Himalaya's consensual abyss.

Moods and Qualities

In the same way pigeons leave their wire
perch, the sheen of moonlight feathers
shadows in the garden. Almost full,
or waning?

On another day the day-moon shines—
a swan made of oil, a summer lamp,
a sign that says how wrong the light can be.

We're always better or worse than ourselves—
the self a mood, tenuous at best. The body
ever-changing in its garment.
Soiled by words, cleansed by silence.

Like the man in the orange caterpillar
set down in a suburban yard, dozing.
His head not quite bobbing.

When did futility seep into man? Slowly,
at first, then settling into his arms and hands.

Rage palpable to animals: the horse spooked
by the man's approach, the chickens ashamed
of laying green eggs.

On bullet trains bent toward Paris
or Berlin the man will count his money
and find it lacking.

In houses filled with windows,
a woman tends her nest of down
or chenille. Inconstancy the breed of man,
constancy the brand of woman.

And the pigeons? When the raven comes,
they scatter as if one mind ruled the flock.

In Squalor

Maybe you forgot
that you too were born
in that place, and sweated all night
in a room with siblings so close to your face
their breath became your own.

Perhaps that night was long
and useless in its humidity.
Objects were alive then—
the cup, the plate, the place settings
rust-smudged and oil-stained.

There was a sitter.
Her name is lost among heaps
of clothing neither clean nor dirty,
shirts in limbo waiting for their destiny,
sheets draped and pleated

by bodies that came and went
and never made up a bed.
Fevers grew in that place,
and with them, delirium, pavement,
pillow casings sewn tight with thread

unraveling during the long hours
of an afternoon spent with a library book.
What did you own? Certain colors,
a crayon ground to a stub.
Piles of newspaper

gone gray on a counter
where mold grew and roaches,
quick-witted, scattered when a naked bulb
found them among crumbs.
Maybe you forgot to forget

and went back home
without meaning to, and saw the same
faces stare back at you without words.
It couldn't be helped, you said to them,
as pipes gurgled and froze.

One day you found snow
sifting in, a drift
six feet tall waiting patiently
as a neighbor on the door sill
for you to answer

its peculiar silence.
Remember how you opened
your life like an envelope
one still morning
to bring in a bottle of milk?

The bottle green,
a centimeter of cream frozen
at the top, and you
there in hand-me-downs,
the only clothes that fit.

—**3**—

Hope grieves between cotton.

César Vallejo, *Trilce XXXI*

Burnt Offering

Not this day, perfect in length
and attitude. The gesture of a figure
emerging from its draperies,
still linked at the elbow and knee
with the past.

Not these crumbs, hoarded
like wheat money in a pantry
the light doesn't penetrate.
A closet like the body,
the flat black recesses of organ

and flowery designs of bone,
the liver smiling with bile.
I can hardly remember summer.
I will give up something else—
the tune of a bird allowing

itself to be eaten, so that a cat
becomes its song, unwittingly
loosening feathers afterwards
in all the right places.
Tools for a devout woman

who will turn her cupboards
upside down to search for one seed
of rye or barley. A tear of jam
burning on an element,
deposits of beer and ice cream.

Chunks of stale bread my children found
when they were searching
for history by candlelight.
Inks, glue, toothpaste, the grain
lodged in cider. That which sours

because it has been forgotten.
Thick walls of a conversation
where my parents sit and talk,
she stirring patience
to the consistency of syrup,

he asserting the argument in gravel notes.
All these fragments,
and others that state their desires
whenever we sweep out our houses,
and the dust catches in our throats.

Lisa's Dress

My daughter, my captive,
is trapped inside a holiday
with me, so we sew a dress.
She wants bridal lace
for the overskirt, and calico beneath—
green bars spaced evenly
for horses, sheep, and geese.

It would be easy
to make her into the one
who carries me along in an unceasing stream
of petite demands—glasses to be filled
and dust to be lifted from its ledges
all day long.

We walk through long rows
of women whose skirts brush the ground.
A cloud dangles corset strings
outside our window.
She is earnest,
her head leaning into the one light
of the machine, her feet
pumping the treadle of imagination.

So that the women
of those days are not forgotten
or lost on her slight figure, we talk
until their dresses ballast
and rise, seams
still tapering to nothing.

They will come and go
the whole afternoon,
now that the past has been mentioned
by the drop of blood swelling from a pinprick.
And I would become one of them,
for her sake.

For the measure of an instant,
surrounded by dressmaker's chalk and tissue,
I'd grow nearsighted
with the sheer weight
of each detail: the stitch that wears the needle out,
the ripper with its scythe of light.

Goaded

Again the old sounds,
the chirrup of cricket & katydid,
& you lost in the forest like Gretel.

Grown up bears lurking.
Johns & whores.
You wander from stump to stump.

Find the trunk of an elephant waving.
The elephant rocks back & forth in a rhythm,
threading figure-eights

with his wrinkled gray-clay body.
Dirt sifts into the light.
Le pauvre, you think to yourself,

and walk on to find the tiger
from Malaysia—one of a hundred left.
A female who does all the work

for her kind. Inside an underground cage
the retired male roars in his low cough,
his frustration at being kept

from her mother.

The Succulents

Forged of exposure, bred to make much
of little. Color comes
from dew, flowers
from a drop of rain.

*

I remember red, the shock of violet,
the yoked egg,
the dream of drowning
on salt grass—
all woven, parted, pleated. Intrigue
as thickly hand-hooked
as a Persian carpet.

*

Or, roots waxed, bleeding color from the earth,
a field of succulents contains
impressionism. Each alizarin, each point
wedded to its own risen cliff.

*

How many rubbery roses have sprouted
close by, ground-hugging.
How hardy the hostess,
how big the rosette, a fluted cabbage.
How make do with less? How grow low
to the ground, keep a profile, remain alpine?

*

Thick stems ramble freely
along a stone wall—plantlets
bound—chick to hen. Purple-cornered,
thrashed by sun.

*

My children gave me this plant
pressed flat against the earth.
It's not much but how it hurts,
the spines greedy for dew,
the fat-fingered fact
of its presence nesting underfoot.

*

And when at last
the house grows quiet,
the container plant
not over-watered,
it's then I come to wonder.

*

In hills and valleys falling
toward the ocean—
oncoming, wave upon wave,
I see the madness of release—
these fat plants rushing inland.

The Courtyard

Never forget winter:
      when it began
and when it will end.

Don't pretend
eastern trees unfurl new leaves
      when ice, pockmarked,
            blackens
a bit of cement, and ice
winds around a corner
      looking for the old woman
who will slip
      and break her hip.

Better to wear a mask
Make-up takes to your face
      as if it had been waiting
all cooped up
      in little bottles
      with French names.

A patent pink
at the tip of the soft brush
wanting to stroke
      your cheek bone.

It's true you might find
a bit of beauty sleep
        left behind in your bed.

        Never forget the scenery
of nightmare—
        that horse ridden
like a piece of luggage
over the curve of red earth.

To live at the equator.
To quell
the centipede,
        the scorpion, the black widow,
and all others who occupy
        this penthouse
                whose windows gaze
upon the chlorine blue
        of a pool
                where, each afternoon
after four o'clock
the odalisques come
        to ply their wares.

Atonement

Why were amends stuck
like bones of a fish in your throat,
why the idea of sin, and whatever black shards
it carries? Tar or sap, you rub your hands

of the coming cold, but it doesn't come off.
What's left behind has a taste
you can pinpoint—almost blood,
the salt of it, almost bitter—the alcohol

of the perpetrator. The moon forgives
the sun for keeping it up nights, moves
in and out of whatever branch seems lenient
enough to give the right cover—not so much

nor so little. A puff of wind could put
it all out—your life, his life, hers, the old man
who has hallucinations.
Who paid first, and how much

did they offer the pale face behind the grid?
Were the penitents right to smear their faces
with soot? The moon never answers questions.
Its sole mission—to glide past,

to seem to rise or set
while hovering on that wing
of your past, exactly as if the number line
held more than imaginary points.

The moon: a zero as fragrant
as the perfume you walked past and wanted
after the woman wearing it had vanished.
That poise equals a problem

more potent than any words,
more buoyant than any wool jacket
with elbow patches—
the one used to placate aging,

the one used to implicate learning.

Israel

He walked down the stairs on his hands.
Continued onto the faded
porch. Laurentian summer. The wasps
already picnicking on flesh,
preying on middle-aged madams—

those who'd rather wear skirted swim
suits and long dresses to hide veins
snaking up their legs, down their arms.
He would have walked upside-down
all the way home. In the restaurant

the woman had gallon soup pots washed
and ready on the stove. Frying
pans oiled to cook a fish that would
never feed more than one man—his
highness, his closed mouth, his gray-blue

eyes taking it all in: gawkers
and wannabe's, roadies for whom
a simple handstand meant too much.
He was used to silence. Why else
the bald head, strong-necked? To balance

death with hope? As if there'd not been
the pogroms, the shame of others
who wouldn't sit down in the Υ
and say *I'm Michael Romanoff,*
Russian Orthodox in my faith

that you will allow me to join
your club. Why the Popeye biceps
and barrel chest on this short man
who would be king
of nothing, row a boat, smile

for any occasion. All the aunts,
great-aunts, curled around him.
Vying to get words in edgewise.
Parting like the Red Sea when he
rose to pick up the check and leave.

The Young Widow

After he died she knew he'd gone out
into space—what kind of space, or where,
she wasn't certain. She kept thinking
if only I had been there I could have stopped
the accident...

After his death she found herself
at the intersection again and again
with the same thought—*if only I had been*
there I could have stopped..., and she stopped
herself from thinking that.

It was as if he'd been dispersed. They married
young, and he had gone to another place.
Perhaps a galaxy—Andromeda,
or the Horsehead nebula in Orion's belt.
They were only in their twenties.

She returned to work.
When the thoughts visited
she made them feel unwelcome,
and finally they left as well, and she
went back to her high-school sweetheart.

These things happen every day:
the two children, the well-appointed house,
even that divorce, messy but behind her now.
Where he went remains an open question,
one she can no longer remember asking.

Windfall

Is it lucky to find apples
lying half-soft
on the grounds of Paradise—
an apple tree,
a field unplanted?
Where is the heart of luck

if not in these late fruits
left to rot? When luck
runs out, is it replaced by illness?
The three-year old
asking *why* all day long
in her hoarse, Sarah Bernhardt voice—

is she happy?
Is it worthwhile to wonder
over a sudden acquisition,
as one might suspect
a green thoroughbred from the track
sold for a cent?

The fruit remains
where it falls. Already
winds blows, heady with autumnal

equinox. Day and night equal
as the algebraic equation
one must solve.

Pears too, reddened
as if stroked by sun,
have left their branches.
They lie over-ripe, useless
except to white insects.
Do white insects hold any purpose

other than to startle
the woman who peers out
from dark pupils
in a face indistinguishable
from other faces?
Is it lucky to find apples

blown from the tree?
What kind of luck
makes a man lose a job?
Is his work then
to be endless, unlocked?
Where pears and apples

meet on a blue road,
and maggots move in overnight
to feast, is that a good place
to have a house built?
Into what world
have we been driven then?

Crabapples

Their skin done
in burgundy and wine,
almost as dark as winter,
below a tree woven
tight as a nest.

Like spikes of fencing,
the same that kept
Rapunzel's suitor
from climbing
her long, thick braid.

Always the fairy tale ending
dangles: a whip or a carrot,
something to trot after
while you are young.
What knot or cloud

of inclusion held
within yellow flesh
makes you so averse
to gathering these stragglers?
Would a peasant appetite

allow the sours to linger
on your black tongue?
Stunted branches
ingrown, thorned stars
strewn across sky glow

in place of the Milky Way.
Entanglement breeds mutation.
When all along I thought
I was the pretty one.

The Rustling

You who are my wind,
the hole in the fabric
of an afternoon,
the winding place
where dresses made from calico
whisper on hangers—
you who compose morning's
spidered windows, prism-cast,
lengths of webbing and droplets...

*

There, the scattered choir
of chimes, crows laughing,
breezeways full of what's gone,
no words to name
this brand of quiet.

*

When I was empty, the quail ran,
their white crests bobbing,
their alarm contagious.

*

Your dress kept in a chest
in the attic with the others.
All antiques speak of mold,
blue willows and sepia. Glass yellowed
by decades, wood scarred
and covered with what the old maids
made as they rocked
and talked: off-white doilies.

*

Were lamps upturned
in the house
where trauma lived?

*

You whose legs are white,
unmarked by weather—
I'll mother you a second time.
I learned a long time ago
the body goes loose
once the tantrum passes.

*

Once, running around a corner,
we knocked into one another.
Your blue eyes told
of the Ukraine,
yet you carried seeds from many countries.

*

Crying from that fall,
I felt your shoulders. Blades
too strong for such a little girl.

*

That night I saw the wing outstretched,
silvered by summer's long twilight,
sifting through blankets
I'd pinned to windows
to keep you asleep.

In the Doghouse

Again, my head rubbing the ceiling
like another Alice who drank
the wrong potion or took too many pills
of different colors, I can feel,
with the stoop in my back,
how long it will be before I'm let out
to breathe scents of spring.

In here with nothing but the smell
of old carpet, of sheets never washed.
The scrappy tennis ball cornered
for good, yellowed with age.
A sepia print of myself,
the guilt-stamps I collected
arrayed like tattoos.

Cold seeps in, sun clips horizon.
Repulsed by my own doggedness,
my desire to please, I settle in
for the longest night, where stars
glitter like treats and jewels. Gifts
so obdurate I know they're mine
if only light years ago.

Restraint

Not Pandora's box, that old trouble
opened yet again for the sake of a script
memorized in childhood. Nor the abominations
of a father who never understood
the pleasures of girlhood. Who raged against
his daughters' fancies. Again, not a genie
in a bottle, nor an apostle of delight and whimsy.
Not even the tiniest portion of a bear claw
slathered with almonds and icing. What
the body holds back comes only in the form
of a rope. A rope and a trapeze. A rope
and a trapeze and a circus artist whose curls
diffuse with light. Her arms extended,
she climbs above the audience, drapes herself
in a shawl of beautiful poses, pouts, falls
deliberately into the trap of hanging upside-down.
When the muses and nymphs fly out
of the box, jar, circus tent, what a ruckus
can be heard for miles as all the birds
and distant relatives of silk monkeys begin
to wake from their century of slumber in the baobab.

Notes

Epigraphs for part breaks are taken from César Vallejo, *Trilce*, translated by Rebecca Seiferle. The Sheep Meadow Press, NY, 1992.

"The Child's Pose" refers to a yoga position.

"Kafka's Wound" was inspired by The Sons: Kafka, Franz. The Sons. Schocken Books Inc., 1989. Transl. Edwin and Willa Muir, with assistance from Mark Harmon and Arthur S. Wensinger.

"Die Kinder" means "the children" in German.

In "Ariel Commands," Ariel is a spirit or shade who appears in Shakespeare's play The Tempest. Ariel is bound to serve the magician Prospero, who rescued him from the tree in which he was imprisoned by Sycroax, the witch who previously inhabited the island.

In "Ah, Vallejo," Hippodamia is a Greek mythological figure. She is the daughter of King Oenomaus of Pisa and Evarete of Argos. The courtship of Hippodamia is associated with chariot races and animal husbandry taboos.

In the poem "Mis en Abyme," the term "Perestroika" refers to the policy of reconstructing the economy and bureaucracy of the former Soviet Union under the leadership of Mikhail Gorbachov in the mid 1980's.

"Winter Burlesque" refers a scene from the movie The Graduate, starring Dustin Hoffman as newly graduated character Ben.

In "The Green Hour," the word "milliner," a maker of hats, was first recorded in reference to the hat. "La fée verte" means "the green fairy" in French. In historical literature this phrase refers to absinthe, which traditionally has a natural green color.

In "Lethe as Mass" the word "rimon" means pomegranate in Hebrew.

"Goaded" was written after visiting Discovery Park in Tacoma, Washington.

"Israel" was written in memory of my grandfather. The story of Michael Romanoff is true. Michael Romanoff (sometimes spelled 'Romanov') was an early Russian Tsar.

"The Young Widow" is dedicated to Erika Carter.

"The Succulents" was inspired by a trip to Point Reyes, outside San Francisco.

About the Author

JUDITH SKILLMAN was born in Syracuse, New York, of Canadian parents, and has dual citizenship. She is an amateur violinist, the mother of three grown children, and the "Grammy" of twin girls. She holds a Masters in English Literature from the University of Maryland, and has taught at the University of Phoenix, Richard Hugo House, City University, and Yellow Wood Academy.

Ms. Skillman is the recipient of an Eric Mathieu King Fund Award from the Academy of American Poets for her book *Storm* (Blue Begonia Press), a King County Arts Commission (KCAC) Publication Prize, Public Arts Grant, and Washington State Arts Commission Writer's Fellowship.

Her poems have appeared in *Poetry, FIELD, The Southern Review, The Iowa Review, Midwest Quarterly Review, Seneca Review, Prairie Schooner, New Poets of the American West,* and other journals and anthologies. Skillman's collaborative translations have appeared in *Northwest Review, BEACONS,* and *Ezra.* She has been a Writer in Residence at the Centrum Foundation in Port Townsend, Washington, and The Hedgebrook Foundation. At the Center for French Translation in Seneffe, Belgium, she translated French Belgian poet Anne-Marie Derèse.

A Jack Straw Writer in 2008 and 2013, Skillman's work has been nominated for Pushcart Prizes, the UK Kit Award, Best of the Web, and is included in *Best Indie Verse of New England.* Visit *www.judithskillman.com*

Other Titles by Judith Skillman:

Angles of Separation, Glass Lyre Press 2014

Broken Lines—The Art & Craft of Poetry, Lummox Press 2013

The Phoenix, New & Selected Poems 2007 – 2013, Dream Horse Press 2013

The White Cypress, Cervéna Barva Press, 2011

The Never, Dream Horse Press, 2010

Prisoner of the Swifts, Ahadada Books, 2009

Anne Marie Derèse in Translation & The Green Parrot, Ahadada Books, 2008

The Body of Pain, Lily Press, 2007

Heat Lightning: New and Selected Poems 1986 – 2006, Silverfish Review Press, 2006

Coppelia, Certain Digressions, David Robert Books, 2006

Opulescence, David Robert Books, 2005

Latticework, David Robert Books, 2004

Circe's Island, Silverfish Review Press, 2003

Red Town, Silverfish Review Press, 2001

Sweetbrier, Blue Begonia Working Signs Series, 2001

Storm, Blue Begonia Press, 1998

Beethoven and the Birds, Blue Begonia Press, 1996

Worship of the Visible Spectrum, Breitenbush Books, 1988

Poetry Books from *Pleasure Boat Studio: A Literary Press:*
Listed chronologically by release date:

The Juried Heart * James Clarke * $17
The Whiskey Epiphanies * Dick Bakken * $17
For My Father * Amira Thoron * $17
Return to a Place Like Seeing * John Palmer * $17
Ascendance * Tim McNulty * $16
Alter Mundus * Lucia Gizzino * trans. from Italian by Michael Daley *
    $15.95
The Every Day * Sarah Plimpton * $15.95
A Taste * Morty Schiff * $15.95
Dark Square * Peter Marcus * $14.95
Notes from Disappearing Lake * Robert Sund * $15
Taos Mountain * Paintings and poetry * Robert Sund * $45 (hardback
    only)
A Path to the Sea * Liliana Ursu, trans. from Romanian by Adam J.
    Sorkin and Tess Gallagher * $15.95
Songs from a Yahi Bow: Poems about Ishi * Yusef Komanyakaa, Mike
    O'Connor, Scott Ezell * $13.95
Beautiful Passing Lives * Edward Harkness * $15
Immortality * Mike O'Connor * $16
Painting Brooklyn * Paintings by Nina Talbot, Poetry by Esther Cohen
    * $20
Ghost Farm * Pamela Stewart * $13
Unknown Places * Peter Kantor, trans. from Hungarian by Michael
    Blumenthal * $14
Moonlight in the Redemptive Forest * Michael Daley * includes a CD *
    $16
Jew's Harp * Walter Hess * $14
The Light on Our Faces * Lee Whitman-Raymond * $13
God Is a Tree, and Other Middle-Age Prayers * Esther Cohen * $10
Home & Away: The Old Town Poems * Kevin Miller * $15
Against Romance * Michael Blumenthal * $14
Days We Would Rather Know * Michael Blumenthal * $14
Craving Water * Mary Lou Sanelli * $15
When the Tiger Weeps * Mike O'Connor * with prose * 15
Concentricity * Sheila E. Murphy * $13.95
The Immigrant's Table * Mary Lou Sanelli * with recipes * $14

Women in the Garden * Mary Lou Sanelli * $14
Saying the Necessary * Edward Harkness * $14
Nature Lovers * Charles Potts * $10
The Politics of My Heart * William Slaughter * $13
The Rape Poems * Frances Driscoll * $13

* * *

The following books are from *Empty Bowl Press*, a Division of
Pleasure Boat Studio:

Hanoi Rhapsodies * Scott Ezell * $10
P'u Ming's Oxherding Pictures & Verses * trans. from Chinese by Red
    Pine * $15
Swimming the Colorado * Denise Banker * $16
Lessons Learned * Finn Wilcox * $10
Petroglyph Americana * Scott Ezell * $15
Old Tale Road * Andrew Schelling * $15
Working the Woods, Working the Sea * Eds. Finn Wilcox, Jerry Gorsline
    * $22
The Blossoms Are Ghosts at the Wedding * Tom Jay * with essays * $15
Desire * Jody Aliesan * $14
Dreams of the Hand * Susan Goldwitz * $14
The Basin: Poems from a Chinese Province * Mike O'Connor * $10 /
    $20 (paper/ hardbound)
The Straits * Michael Daley * $10
In Our Hearts and Minds: The Northwest and Central America * Ed.
    Michael Daley * $12 * with prose
The Rainshadow * Mike O'Connor * $16
Untold Stories * William Slaughter * $10 / $20 (paper / hardbound)

* * *

Our Chapbook Series:

No. 1: *The Handful of Seeds: Three and a Half Essays* * Andrew
    Schelling * $7 * essays
No. 2: *Original Sin* * Michael Daley * $8

No. 3: *Too Small to Hold You* * Kate Reavey * $8

No. 4: *The Light on Our Faces* – re-issued in non-chapbook (see above list)

No. 5: **Eye** * William Bridges * $8

No. 6: *Selected* **New Poems** *of Rainer Maria Rilke* * trans. fm German by Alice Derry * $10

No. 7: *Through High Still Air: A Season at Sourdough Mountain* * Tim McNulty * $9 * with prose

No. 8: *Sight Progress* * Zhang Er, trans. fm Chinese by Rachel Levitsky * $9 * prosepoems

No. 9: *The Perfect Hour* * Blas Falconer * $9

No. 10: *Fervor* * Zaedryn Meade * $10

No. 11: *Some Ducks* * Tim McNulty * $10

No. 12: *Late August* * Barbara Brackney * $10

No. 13: *The Right to Live Poetically* * Emily Haines * $9

* * *

From other publishers (in limited editions):

In Blue Mountain Dusk * Tim McNulty * $12.95 * a Broken Moon Press book

China Basin * Clemens Starck * $13.95 * a Story Line Press book

Journeyman's Wages * Clemens Starck * $10.95 * a Story Line Press book

* * *

Orders: Pleasure Boat Studio books are available by order from your bookstore, directly from our website, or through the following:

SPD (Small Press Distribution) Tel. 8008697553, Fax 5105240852

Partners/West Tel. 4252278486, Fax 4252042448

Baker & Taylor 8007751100, Fax 8007757480

Ingram Tel 6157935000, Fax 6152875429

Amazon.com or **Barnesandnoble.com**

Pleasure Boat Studio: A Literary Press
201 West 89th Street
New York, NY 10024
www.pleasureboatstudio.com / *pleasboat@nyc.rr.com*